Teasing Mom

Story by Annette Smith

Illustrations by Naomi C. Lewis

One Saturday morning, Mom said,
"It's going to be hot, today
and the ground is very dry.
I will water the garden now."

"We will help you," said Matthew.

He ran to get the hose.

He hooked it up

and turned it on.

"Matthew!" called Mom.

"Turn the water down, please.

It's coming out too fast."

Matthew went back
and turned it down.
The water came out slowly.

"That's better," called Mom.

"Oh, no!" said Mom.

"The hose is stuck under that rock, and the water can't come out."

Emma ran across to the hose, and she moved it away from the rock.

Matthew looked at the hose,
and he looked over at Mom.

"I will trick Mom," he said,
and he ran and hid by the shed.

Mom was still watering the flowers.

Matthew put his foot down on the hose.
The water stopped.

"The hose is stuck **again**," said Emma.
"I will go and fix it for you, Mom."

Whoosh!

"Oh, Emma! Look at me,"
said Mom. "I'm all wet."

"Mom, the hose was not stuck at all," said Emma.

"Look over there at Matthew. He played a trick on you."

"Come on, Emma," said Mom. "We will get him."

Mom and Emma were laughing as they ran after Matthew.

He tried to run past them.
He wanted to get inside the house, but he was too late.

Whoosh!

"Now we are **all** wet," laughed Matthew.